Hydroponics

*Hydroponic Gardening Guide
From Beginner To Expert*

Thomas Thatcher

Thomas Thatcher

Free Bonus!!!

We would like to offer you our FREE Guide to jump-start you on a path to improve your life & Exclusive access to our Breakthrough Book Club!!! It's a place where we offer a NEW FREE E-book every week! Also our members are actively discussing, reviewing, and sharing their thoughts on the Book of The Week and on topics to help each other Breakthrough Life's Obstacles! With a Chance to win a $25 Gift Card EVERY Month! Please Enjoy Your FREE Guide & Access to the **Breakthrough Book Club**

https://publishfs.leadpages.co/the-breakthrough-book-club-d/

Thomas Thatcher

Table of Contents

Thomas Thatcher

Introduction

Hydroponics is the method of growing plants without soil by supplying them with a constant nutrient solution. Despite the fact that this method remains fairly unknown outside of a small sector of the horticultural world it has in fact been around for a long time. It is a system that was used extensively in the hanging gardens of Babylon and has been studied extensively by scientists and horticulturists for the last several hundred years.

There are many powerful reasons for commercial food growers to use this method but it is also now being used more frequently by the domestic gardener keen to produce a high yield in a small amount of space. Though it is seen primarily as a way of producing crops for the table it is also a method that can be used for the production of ornamental plants.

All plants require air, light, and dissolved nutrients to grow. Hydroponics allows for a very precisely controlled amount of nutrients, dissolved in water, to be administered directly to the root system, as the plant requires it. Because the root system is no longer obliged to spread so far in order to attain the nutrients it requires this in turn enables the grower to plant his crops at much higher densities which is just one reason why hydroponic crop yields are so much greater than the more traditional soil planted yields.

There are a variety of variations on the hydroponic theme and this book will take a look at the main options the gardener has available to them. Though some of the methods might sound overly complicated for the home gardener I advise you to persist because what at first might appear a difficult system to reproduce is in fact surprisingly easy in many cases and the increase in yields will be staggering. You have been given a great deal of information on the different types of systems that have been used often by numerous people. You have been given a detailed description on how to construct, maintain and care for each of these systems.

Since you are a beginner, there is a possibility that you may make a mistake. It is OK to make a mistake since failures are the stepping-stones to success. Keep forging ahead! I hope you enjoy the book.

Thomas Thatcher

Chapter 1

A Little History and Some Basic Principals

Primitive forms of hydroponics have been carried on by various societies for thousands of years. The word hydroponic itself stems from an amalgamation of two Ancient Greek words, 'hydro' for water and 'ponic' for work. In other words, the water was supposed to do the work that had created such toil for mankind ever since he began to practice agriculture.

Various forms of it have been carried on in Kashmir for centuries and one group, the Aztecs of America, developed a form of floating garden. Pushed to the marshy regions of Lake Tenochtitlan, in what is now Mexico, by other more aggressive tribes these nomadic people were forced to come up with a viable agricultural system in order to survive. They developed a system of floating rafts woven together out of reeds that eventually turned in to an archipelago of floating islands. These islands teemed with vegetables, flowers and even trees. The historian William Prescott recorded the destruction of the Aztec empire by the colonizing Spaniards and he described the floating gardens as 'Wondering islands of Verdure, teeming with flowers and vegetables and moving like rafts on the water.'

Many historians believe that hydroponics was an important ingredient in the creation of the famous hanging gardens of Babylon, which was one of the seven wonders of the Ancient World. If that is the case this is probably the first example of hydroponics being used as a farming method.

In more modern times the first scientific studies took place in the 1600s when the Belgian Jan van Helmont demonstrated that you could grow a willow in a tube containing 200 pounds of dried soil and fed only with rainwater. After five years the willow shoot had obtained a weight of 160 pounds whilst the soil had only decreased in weight by two ounces. He concluded that plants obtain what they require for growth from water. Whilst partially correct in his assumptions, that early demonstration failed to take into account the need for carbon dioxide and oxygen, which are also crucial to plant development.

In 1699 John Woodwards took the experiment a stage further when he grew plants in water, which contained differing amounts of diluted soil. The plants that had the highest concentrates of soil grew best. In this early version of the manmade hydroponic solution Woodwards realized that soil probably contained some nutrient crucial to plant growth but with chemistry not yet discovered he was unable to identify what those nutrients were.

Science began to gather momentum in the decades that followed and scientist were able to prove that plants absorbed water via their roots and that this then passed through their systems to be released through pores in the leaves. They also discovered that the roots also draw up nutrients and oxygen and that leaves draw carbon dioxide from the air.

In 1851 French scientist Jean Baptist Boussingault began experimenting with inert growing media and water with various combinations of elements available in soil. In 1860 the first nutrient solution in which plants could be grown was published by Professor Julius von Sachs. Various solutions continued to be developed but at this stage all studies had been based around laboratory research. It was not until the 1920's that Doctor William Gericke began to extend lab work to include outdoor crop production. In the process he termed the use of the word hydroponics and laid the groundwork for all forms of modern day hydroponics, as we know it. Developments continued of course, and still today this is an evolving science but we now have a far better handle on the methodology of growing plants without the use of soil.

There are several major benefits to using this method to cultivate plants. We immediately eliminate soil borne pests and diseases. Greater control over the plants provides more consistent size and production. Water waste is massively reduced since the water is reused. Crops mature more rapidly often allowing for two crops per year where only one is possible in traditional soil growing systems and finally greater yields are produced. In a world with decreasing natural resources and a rapidly increasing population growth it is almost inevitable that this will be an area of agricultural production that sees massive growth.

Gericke had proved that it was not soil that plants needed, it was the nutrients and moisture that the soil contained along with adequate plant support. This could be provided just as, and possibly even more effectively, by adding the exact nutrient requirements to the water and then growing the plant in an inert medium purely for stability and support. In the soil nutrients tend to be leached away from the plant roots thus forcing the plant to continuously extend its root system in an effort to reach them. Nutrients can be replaced but it is difficult to estimate the exact requirements a plant has in a system where the leaching cannot be controlled or measured accurately. This creates a further disadvantage in that the plant must waste valuable energy in root production that could be diverted to crop production. When growing in soil, the root system draws up nutrients and acts as an as an anchor and support for the plant. Provided the plant is given plenty of nutrients then the root system can be considerably smaller and the anchorage function can take place in any non-leaching material. Some hydroponic systems do away with the planting medium altogether and suspend the plant, feeding the trailing roots by a mist system. This method is perfectly successful.

Gericke's initial systems soon proved too technical for most would be hydroponic growers. One of the main problems lay in keeping a consistent supply of oxygen in the nutrient solution. Interest in the methods he developed had been triggered, however, and since then ongoing developments have made hydroponics more and simpler. Now there are huge greenhouse producers throughout the world producing very high yields. There are now over 1000 000 soil-less household units in the USA. The need to develop this system is demonstrated by these figures: in 1950 there were 3.7 million acres of land being cultivated and a population of just under 151 000 000 people. Today that population has soared to 204 000 000 and the amount of land under cultivation dropped to 3.2 million acres. With figures like this it becomes apparent that the need for viable crop production to increase and it is likely that there will be less land available for it to increase in.

Rooftops are one area that are being looked at and utilized more and more. Vast flat surfaces within city confines offer a perfect place to produce crops. What is more when we start to produce crops within urban environments we dramatically reduce the amount of mileage that the crops must travel in order to get to the end user with knock on benefits, both in terms of pollution created and freshness of the end product.

Modern hydroponics can go even smaller scale than that though. Nowadays it is easy for a homeowner to set up his own hydroponic garden in the back yard and there are even smaller units being designed for kitchens and apartments. The main requirements of water and electricity are already in place in these situations. At its most basic level here is what you will need to make your own unit.

A growing chamber or tray. This will contain the growing medium and plant roots and can be anything that holds water and is big enough for the plants you want to grow.

A reservoir. This will contain the water and nutrient system that will then be pumped to the growing chamber in a cyclical action. Once again, it can be made of just about anything as long as it holds sufficient liquid. It should, however, be light proof so as to inhibit the growth of algae and microorganisms.

A submersible pump. This does not need to be expensive and pumps the water from the reservoir to the growing chamber and back again. Fishpond pumps are often used.

Some method of delivery. This is just a system to convey the solution from the reservoir to the chamber. PVC tubing works perfectly well.

Already you have the basis for a basic but functional system. A timer is one addition that would make your life easier and costs very little. This will switch the pump on and off and ensure that the roots of the plant are always kept moist. An air pump, even one as simple as you see in small fish tanks, will help keep the solution oxygenated which is essential to plant growth and will also ensure the nutrients circulating evenly. The air pump is normally situated in the reservoir. Remember that roots need to be kept in the dark to perform at their best so depending on what growing medium you use it may be necessary to cover them in some way.

Grow lights are another addition that will give you greater control and increase the optimum growing period but these are not necessary in the most basic units. If you do opt for grow lights you may want to consider an additional timer for those.

This very basic system can be made at home or purchased as a premade kit. There are even examples of people making a system by stringing plastic soda bottles across an apartment window then linking them with PVC tubing and pumping the nutrient solution around with very good results.

The point I am trying to make is that this method of plant production is no longer restricted solely to large-scale professional outfits. There is little point in growing your own vegetables if your startup cost is such that each tomato you produce owes you twenty dollars.

Thomas Thatcher

Chapter 2

Facts About the Hydroponic System

You have been told a little about the history of the hydroponics system. Let us try to learn a little more about the hydroponic system. The systems uses water as its base, but before we go into the intricate details of the system, let us try to understand why you need to use water instead of another solvent. Imagine if the earth has absolutely no water on it. Do you think you would have been able to survive on such a planet? Would there be a way for you to quench your thirst? There are numerous probes being run into finding water on other planets when there is enough water on our planet.

Every organism right from a tiny organism to a large organism always looks for water. This is because of the fact that the organisms crave for water since they have always been around water. Well, the book has a lot of information about water! You will be able to learn about the different ways you can use the sources of water around you instead of having to waste the source. When you use these sources of water along with the nutrient powders, you will find your plants extremely well in your very own garden.

You have to remember that water and fire never work together at all, but they work tremendously well when it comes to plants. If there is a forest that has been burnt down or even a tree has been burnt down, the wood turns to ash. This ash contains lot of potassium, which is an extremely important mineral for the growth of the plants. Once the water touches this ash, you will find that the potassium from the ash moves into the soil and is absorbed by the roots of the plants. Any other leaves or branches that have been decayed will be decomposed by microorganisms. The microorganisms also excrete the organic waste after consuming the dead leaves and branches. This waste also contains a lot of minerals that the plants crave for. The water helps in converting these minerals into their diluted forms that would make it easier for the plants to absorb the minerals.

If you were trying to identify the different ways you would be able to make certain that the plants in your hydroponic system have been able to obtain all the minerals they need. If this happens, you will be able to ensure that the elements in nature are able to live in perfect harmony with each other. The forests and the trees need to burn in order to ensure that the microorganisms and other insects eat well. This would mean that the monsoon would need to wash away all the nutrients from the organic waste and the minerals from the ash. This is a system that you would never find anywhere except for the rainforest.

Hydroponic systems are the perfect rainforest in your backyard! They work towards enriching the water in the system with numerous nutrients and salts that are needed in the nature. What you will need to do is create a solution that would provide all the plants with an extremely balanced system. Over the course of this book, you will learn that a hydroponic system contains a solution that is in abundance with the nutrients. The system always helps in protecting these solutions from being turned into vapor! It is for this very reason that you will be able to manage the sources of water in areas that are barren and arid. The system has often been called 'Earth Friendly gardening' and has gained immense popularity over the last few decades.

The hydroponic system is a form of art that is often called water gardening. It is always good to understand the water you will be using in this system better. You will need to know what the contents in the water you will be using. Make sure that you approach a company to understand and analyze every minute detail in the sample of water. If you know the source of the water, you will find it easier to understand and analyze the sample. What is of most importance is that you understand the hardness or the softness of the water you will be using. If the water is found to be very hard, you will find that the water has a high concentration of calcium carbonate. If the water is soft, you will find that the water is in its purest forms. Distilled water or even water that has been cured through osmosis is also in its purest form. You could use a particular nutrient solution if you need but make sure that you know whether or not the water is hard or soft.

Also keep these points in mind when you are trying to purchase a set of nutrients for your solution.

You need to make sure that you do remember that it is plants you are working with. You have to also learn that the plants always absorb the nutrients that they need through their roots. Make sure that you always pay attention to the roots and do not cover them too much with the water. You have to ensure that you always keep in mind that your plants need a lot of oxygen and this is obtained through the roots.

If you are looking at keeping the roots healthy, you will need to ensure that the water always circulates well throughout the system. Make sure that the water is not stagnated since that would kill all your plants. The best part of the system is that you can grow plants of any kind without having to worry too much about the climatic conditions. All you need to do is to ensure that you have the perfect protection and the perfect solutions that are in your hydroponic system. This will ensure that you have an extremely good yield!

Thomas Thatcher

Chapter 3
Hydroponics – A Quick Overview

The hydroponics system is a wonder in modern science! You have to realize that the hydroponics system always tends to have a great yield of fruits, vegetables, flowers, grains, herbs and many other plants too. You may be able to cultivate food you would never have been able to before. The system works wonders when it comes to producing food that is extremely healthy and strong. The food also has a large amount of nutrients which when consumed would leave a human being with immense energy and strength.

The newest techniques of hydroponic systems always help in providing a world with a huge quantity of food that could never be cultivated anywhere else. It has been seen that the cultivation of crops using hydroponics is extremely effective.

It is for this reason that NASA has decided to cultivate crops using this system on certain planets. Only when scientists decided to understand the composition of the nutrients in plants did they understand the science behind the system of hydroponics. You may be surprised to learn the fact that these experiments have been conducted since 1600AD! The records all have the conclusions that the plants have a chance to grow up in a mixture of sand and gravel. The plants do not need soil to grow too! You could use the hanging gardens of Babylon and the floating gardens of the Aztec as classic examples. There are certain parts of Egypt that used the hydroponics systems to cultivate fruits and vegetables.

The year 1936 saw a new word – hydroponics – that was introduced by Dr. W. F. Gericke. This was the word used by him since he described a newer technique of cultivating plants. He had said that plants – various kinds of plants – could be cultivated just in water and nutrients. You will learn a little later about how this word is an apt description of the new art of gardening – hydroponic gardening.

You have been told that the hydroponics gardening method only uses a nutrient solution that will help in keeping the plants healthy and strong. The solutions that are used in this system always surround the roots and help the plant absorb the minerals and vitamins they will need using the forces of gravity. Some of the hydroponic systems use electric pumps while there are others that have the simplest working technique. Any kind of system ensures that the roots of the plants always stay in the nutrient solution that is in the reservoir. It is always good to make sure that the nutrient solution does not stagnate since that would mean the death of your plants!

You will learn that the plants that have been growing in the hydroponics system are in fact strong and healthy when compared with the plants that have been grown using traditional methods. This is because of the fact that the nutrient solution always gives your plants the balanced diet that they need. The system also keeps the plants away from any kind of pest. The systems always help in conserving and managing the sources of water around you. You will also be able to ensure that the water never goes to waste or evaporates when it is used in the system.

If the area you live in is arid or barren, you have to try to look for different ways in which you can grow your crops and hydroponic systems are one of those ways. The hydroponic system always provides your crops with water and the nutrients that your plants will need. Make sure that you grow all the plants together to ensure that you conserve a lot of space too. When the environment you grow your plants in is really clean, you will be able to ensure that the crops are being grown under ideal conditions. You will also be able to save a large amount of money. The best part is that you do not have to go looking for the right soil or even spend any money on the fertilizers and pesticides to increase the yield of the plants.

When you use the conventional methods of farming, you will be able to save immense levels of energy. Your plants would definitely be less healthy when compared to plants that have been cultivated in a hydroponics system. This is because of the fact that the hydroponic system has a lot of nutrients and minerals that the plants need. These minerals are absorbed by the roots of the plants in the system that would ensure that the plants become very healthy and strong.

Plants that have grown in the hydroponic system are always healthier than the ones that have been grown in soil. They always have a lot of energy and health since they always obtain a balanced diet of minerals and vitamins that they will need desperately. The plants are extremely strong during the worst of the climatic conditions too. I hope you have gathered a fair idea on what the hydroponics system is all about. Let us now try to understand the medium you will need to use in the system.

Understanding the growing medium

You have been told numerous times earlier that you need an extremely proper medium to grow your plants since the medium is extremely important for you to obtain a good yield. You could use either a solid or a liquid medium but either should have a set of characteristics that are listed below:

1. The particles of the medium should never be smaller than 2 millimeters. The particles should be between the sizes of 2 – 7 millimeters.

2. The medium should never decompose easily.

3. Make sure that the medium is adept at removing any excess liquid that is in the system while trying to ensure that you maintain the moisture of the plants.

4. Try to ensure that the medium is portable.

5. The medium should be found anywhere – implying that it needs to be readily available!

6. Make sure that the medium always keeps toxic microorganisms away from the humans.

7. Make sure that the medium has not been contaminated or spoilt due to the industrial wastes.

The list given below has the recommended media that you could use!

- 80 percent rice hill: 20 percent saw dust
- 60 percent rice hull: 40 percent sand
- Clean river water
- 60 percent rice hull: 40 percent ground clay bricks
- 50 percent rice hull: 50 percent ground volcanic stones

If you have decided to use the rice hulls, you have to ensure that you wash them well and keep them wet for a minimum of ten days to ensure that the seeds begin to germinate. You have to ensure that these seeds are removed once they have germinated. If you are using sawdust, you have to be extremely careful since there is a possibility that the sawdust may harm the plants. Ensure that you choose the right sawdust. You are given a better idea about the different growing media in the next chapter. Make sure that you use the ones that have been given in the chapter only!

Thomas Thatcher

Chapter 4
Different Growing Mediums

There are many different growing mediums which gardeners and horticulturists all get into the habit of blending to their own requirements so here we shall look at some of the most popular and discuss their advantages and disadvantages. In all cases you are looking for a medium that is light soilless and does not contain nutrients or chemicals that will affect the plant in any way or interfere with the nutrient mix that you are providing. It also needs to be porous enough to facilitate the easy transfer of oxygen and nutrients to the roots. We use these inert planting mediums for two main reasons. They minimize the amount of light reaching the root ball and they provide a support for the plant to grow in.

Probably the three favorite materials that you are likely to come across are coconut coir, perlite and LECA.

Coconut coir

Coconut coir is a byproduct of the coconut industry. It is made of the hairy outer coating that surrounds the coconut shell and prior to being discovered as a useful product for the horticultural trade it was used for little more than stuffing for cheap mattresses. The recognition that the harvesting of peat was causing major environmental problems meant that environmentally concerned growers needed to look for new products to replace peat as a growing medium and coconut coir fitted the bill in many instances. It is sold in blocks and may also be called palm peat or simply coir.

The blocks swell to between six and eight times their compressed size when mixed with water so if you are ordering some don't be too disappointed when they arrive and appear a little smaller than you had hoped. They are particularly good at holding moisture and can absorb up to eight times their own weight. One of the disadvantages of this medium is that because it is so light it has a tendency to be washed about and for this reason is not suitable for ebb and flow systems unless combined with one of the other materials available. Growing mediums can be washed and reused after each crop. The medium is rinsed in diluted bleach then rinsed again and allowed to dry. With coir this system can only be used three or four times before it begins to break down.

Perlite

This is another product that has been around in the horticultural industry for many years. It is made by heating silica flakes that expands into very small and light pieces. These have good moisture retention and are chemically neutral so are favored by makers of potting mixes as it increases moisture holding capacity without adding weight. If cleaned by washing with bleach it can be used many times as a hydroponic planting medium. Its lightweight makes it impossible to use in the ebb and flow system unless combined with something like LECA. It has a good wicking action that makes it one of the favorite choices in wicking systems.

LECA

LECA stands for light expanded clay aggregate and is made by lightly heating clay particles until they expand from anything between six to eighteen millimeters in diameter. It is a lightweight free draining product that is very popular in the indoor plant industry and which you have probably seen used as a mulch on potted plants in shopping centers or offices. It is fairly good at holding moisture but is not on a par with something like coir in this respect and when high water retention is required the two products are often mixed at a fifty - fifty ration. The coir then holds the moisture while the LECA acts as a stabilizer to stop the coir being washed away. In this way you can get the best use from both products. You may decide to experiment on the ratios that work best for you.

These are three of the products you are most likely to come across but there are many others that will work well and you may decide to adapt to one of the products below either because of price or availability.

Vermiculite

A product with many similarities to perlite it looks like mica. It is mined in South Africa, China, Brazil and Zimbabwe. Once mined, the product is expanded by heating in a kiln and becomes very light and water retentive. Like perlite it is often used as a moisture retainer when mixed with potting composts because of it neutral pH and its lightweight. In the hydroponic arena it should be used in its pure form and not mixed with compost or soil. It does not break down and can be reused if correctly cleaned.

Peat Based Soilless Compost

Peat is mad from compressed moss and plant products that have been compressed in the ground for hundreds and even thousands of years. It has been the mainstay of the nursery industry for a very long time but its widespread use has led to a breakdown of much of the local flora and fauna in the associated environments where it is dug and there are now growing calls for its extraction to be banned in favor of more sustainable products such as coir. That said it is an extremely versatile growing medium though if you choose to use it please make sure you get it from a sustainably managed producer.

It has excellent moisture retentive characteristics and is very lightweight. Suppliers often mix it with biofungicides, which are naturally occurring anti-fungal agents, or mycorrhizae that are natural root stimulants.

Rock Wool

Suitable for both ebb and flow and for continuous drip systems rock wool is a versatile growing medium. It retains water well and its porous texture means that it facilitates the free flow of air. It is made from a type of rock that is melted and then spun to produce a material similar to foam. Two factors do need to be borne in mind when choosing this material for your growing medium. Initially it must be soaked overnight to ensure the pH is neutral and secondly it does not break down so disposal can be a problem.

Oasis cubes

This lightweight foam has been used by the florist industry for decades and is ideal for the small-scale hydroponic producer. It can hold up to forty times its own weight in water and still remain breathable. It is ideal for starting both seeds and cuttings and is very workable making it a good product for the simple wick system. These properties can be used in any of the six main growing systems and the pH is neutral.

Other options

So long as the growing medium contains no nutrients and is free draining there are plenty of products that are not related to the horticultural industry that serve well in the hydroponic world and you are free to think out of the box and experiment with whatever ingredients you find that may fit the bill. Those lightweight packaging peanuts you had sitting around in the garage with no real use for, are one example. Builder's sand was used widely in the early days of hydroponics. It needs to be rinsed to leach out any chemicals and it has a low water retention capacity but it does work. Be careful though because it tends to pack down when it has been wet a few times and then drainage will deteriorate.

Gravel is another cheap and easy to find material. It offers no water retention but sometimes both of these qualities might prove desirable. In Australia sawdust is often used for large-scale tomato growing because it retains moisture and is often free. If you decide to experiment with this material make sure it has not been polluted with any products whilst still at the sawmill. They could damage your plants. It does tend to break down but as it is usually free it is easily replaced.

Rice hulls are a bi product of rice farming. They are as effective as perlite though they do decompose so will have a limited life span. As it is usually cheap or free this may not be an issue and regular replacement is recommended, as there tends to be a buildup of salts that are detrimental to plant growth.

What I hope I have demonstrated is that there is no specific product you have to use provided it is pH neutral and drains well. I have heard of instances of people using torn up cardboard, broken brick and tiles and even the stuffing out of an old mattress. Feel free to experiment with whatever comes to hand.

Chapter 5

The Different Hydroponic Systems

Although there is a great deal of variety in the different types of hydroponic systems in essence it comes down to six different types. The drip system, the ebb and flow system, N.F.T., the water culture system, Aeroponics and the wick system. These systems can all be modified to suit the environment and budget of the individual user and the space they have available to them. In choosing an appropriate system for your own needs you need to consider these things as well as the size and types of plant you will be growing. Remember also that systems will need to be cleaned very thoroughly from time to time so look for a unit that you can disassemble and clean easily. The next chapter will help you understand the details behind the different systems that you can use for gardening. Make sure that you choose the right system since you will be able to obtain all the material you will need for that system.

The drip system

This is one of the most popular systems both for the home gardener and the commercial producer. One of the main reasons that it is so popular is that it facilitates the production of large plants. Basically each plant is potted into growing medium in an individual pot. A drip line is then extended from the reservoir to each pot and when the pump is turned on nutrient solution drips into the pots until such time as the medium is soaked through. The excess solution then drains through the pot to where it is captured in a tray that returns it to the reservoir by means of gravity. The timer is set to turn the pump on again just before the medium gets dry so that the roots are kept constantly moist.

In domestic units these systems tend to be circulating but some commercial units are non- circulating. What happens in these larger operations is that when the water drains through the growing medium it is not captured. This may sound wasteful but it relies on the fact that the timer is so accurate that when set correctly it gives enough solution to the growing medium to wet it exactly with very little waste. Just before the medium dries it then adds more solution. The advantage to the commercial grower is twofold. Firstly, he is not required to have a huge area of catchment trays running the solution back to the reservoir and secondly each time he tops up the reservoir he can replace the exact amount of nutrient appropriate to the plant's needs. The nutrients within a system decrease as they are absorbed by the plant and so a circulating system must be checked frequently to measure the nutrient levels. In a non-circulating system the reservoir must be topped up frequently but on large-scale operations there is normally staff in place to see to this.

Ebb and flow system

This is a method that suits the smaller scale of the domestic user either in the house or in the garden because it is easy to build and can be designed to fit into any available space. Plants are potted into a growing medium and placed into a fairly deep tray. An overflow line is connected to the tray at a level of one or two inches below the surface of the growing medium and water is then pumped from the reservoir into the tray. When the water level reaches the overflow it simply runs back to the reservoir. When this starts a float valve turns off the pump. The same valve turns the water back on again when the reservoir refills. In this way the roots of the plant are constantly being submerged in solution and drained again. It is a system that can be made on a really tiny scale and many pre-made systems utilize this method. When building your own system be sure that the overflow pipe is sufficiently large to carry away water faster than it can arrive via the pump.

Nutrient film technique

In this system plants are grown in a matt of material such as rock wool and placed into a tray with a fine film at its base. A pump carries the nutrients through the film and this soaks the film keeping the roots constantly damp. Excess water simply runs back to the reservoir via gravity. Plants are normally planted through some sort of material to keep light from reaching the roots, as there is no growing medium to cover them.

The system can be very small but when used on large-scale operations long channels are filled with film and the same system is just notched up to a greater size. Because of the shallow depth of this system it is most suited to small fast growing crops such as lettuce and certain types of herb. The system is very effective but with small fast growing plants of this nature there is a risk of them dying quickly in the event of the roots drying out so there is little time to respond if there is some sort of breakdown in the system such as electrical failure.

Water culture system

In this system the root is constantly kept wet by the very fine splashing of tiny droplets of nutrient mix. The plants in are suspended with their roots hanging down into the reservoir. Instead of a water pump an air pump is placed into the reservoir and the water aerated at a pressure that will make the water look like it is boiling lightly. Because the top of the roots are just above the nutrient mix level the bubbling effect created by the pump will cause droplets to hit the roots. This system can be as simple as a large plastic bucket with a hole or holes cut into the lid through which the roots are suspended. The air pump is then placed in the bottom of the bucket and the lid put back on. (You may need to cut a groove for the lead to the pump). The most difficult part of the operation is setting the water depth so that it adequately splashes the roots. Don't worry if the lower roots touch the solution as long as there is still plenty of root material exposed to the air. Make sure that the lid is made of a material that will keep the roots in the dark. This method ensures a really well oxygenated mix reaching the roots but it also requires monitoring of the depth of the solution. More sophisticated systems of the water culture system are used commercially but at the same time it is just an upgrade of the system used by the Aztecs that I mentioned at the beginning of this book.

Aeroponics

Another variation of the hydroponic system is called Aeroponics but as you will see the main principals differ very little from the other techniques you have seen so far. Once again the plants are supported above the solution supply only this time the solution is mist sprayed onto the roots. Like with NFT no growing medium is needed. Think of those small fine sprays you have on an ordinary garden irrigation system. Nutrient solution is pumped from the reservoir and instead of going directly to the routes it passes through the sprayers that wet the roots with a fine mist of water. Excess water can then be captured in trays and run back to the reservoir although the spray spreads the water further and so recapturing the nutrient solution is harder. Most commercial units don't attempt to recapture the moisture but instead try to regulate the delivery system so precisely that there is minimal waste.

The wick system

Of all the systems that have been discussed so far this is by far the simplest one. The plants being grown are potted in their growing medium and then suspended above a bucket of nutrient mix. At its most basic you could have a plastic container with a plant inside balanced on a bucket of nutrients. A wicking material is then placed between the growing medium and the nutrient mix. This can be any material that will carry moisture such as a hemp rope, strips of carpet under-felt or some twisted strips of hessian sacking. There are no moving parts, material costs are minimal, if any, and there is very little skill needed to put it all together.

There are however multiple problems with this method. Firstly only small plans should be grown as the wick, even if you use several, will not be able to carry sufficient water to satisfy the needs of a larger plant. Secondly the wick will not transport the nutrients evenly and those left behind in the reservoir will build up to form a residue that could become toxic to the plant. Thirdly there is no oxygenation taking place in the reservoir. This means could be used by a beginner to grow a few small plants as an introduction to other systems of hydroponics. It is also often used by teachers as a means to demonstrate capillary action, as that is what is taking place here. Some people use an L shaped tube to carry water to the bottom of a plants roots. When the water is poured down the pipe it will be carried upwards by capillary action in the growing medium but this is not really hydroponics in its true sense as devised by Dr. William Gerricke.

There is another system called Aquaponic, which is often confused with hydroponics and does in fact have many similarities but it is not regarded as true hydroponics. Aquaponics principals involve using the waste matter created by fish to feed plants with a system very similar to those of hydroponics. Adding nutrients in controlled quantities is so essential to the philosophy behind hydroponics that the two subjects are best considered separately.

Thomas Thatcher

Chapter 6
Understanding the Hydroponic Systems

This chapter will help you understand the different hydroponics systems much better than you did before. You will gather information on the materials and tools you need to construct the systems. You will also be able to learn how you can make any modifications to the system too!

Bubbler System

This system is the simplest of all hydroponic systems that have ever been developed. It is for this very reason that I am going over this system first. You will be able to build your very own unit using the information that has been given in this section. The system is like a water culture system where the roots are all suspended in the nutrient solution. The system uses the nutrients in the solution to give your plants the boost it needs. The system that has been explained here is only for a few plants.

Material Required

You will need to procure these materials in order to ensure that you build the perfect system.

1. A 10-gallon bucket with a lid. It is always good to get darker colors, but if you have a transparent bucket, you will need to spray paint it with a dark shade.

2. An air pump, stone and tubing. These components are extremely important since they help in sending oxygen into the solution. You could use a small air pump if you want to since that would be enough too.

3. A netted cap. You could choose to purchase a netted cap or you could make it on your own. The size of the cap would depend on the number of plants you would like to cultivate in your system.

4. A growing medium. You could use a nominal amount of one of the media that have been mentioned above.

5. A nutrient mix.

Tools Required

1. A hole saw which is used to adjust the sizes of the netted pots.

2. A power drill that is used to cut the holes in the lid.

3. A tape measure to measure the size of the tubing

4. A drill bit that is used to drill holes in the water gauge and the air tubing.

5. A knife

6. Safety glasses

Construction

1. You will have to make holes in the lid to fit the plastic cups into it. When you are doing this, you have to ensure that the plastic cups are durable and have sides that have tapered. Ensure that the hole is large enough to fit the cup firmly. You have to be certain of the fact that the cups do not slip.

2. You will now have to drill a hole that is perfect to fit in the air tube.

3. Now, move the air tubing through the hole and push it all the way to the bottom of the bucket. You will

now have to attach the air stone and leave a few airlines inside the bucket so that the stone will lay flat at the bottom of the bucket.

4. Now fill the bucket with the created nutrient solution. Make sure that the nutrient solution has been prepared according to what crop you will be cultivating. Make sure that it only touches the netted cups and does not submerge them. You will probably have to fill it up with more of the nutrient solution if you are starting with a seed.

5. Cover the bucket with the lid.

6. Once the roots have grown a few inches in the cup, you will need to reduce the level of the nutrient solution at least by an inch at the bottom surface of the plastic cup.

7. Now, hook the other end of the air tube to the air pump and ensure that the nutrient solution begins to bubble.

8. When the bubbles have begun to appear, you will need to place the plant in the netted cups making sure that the roots of the plant only swirl at the

bottom of the cup. Now, fill the bottom of the cup with the medium.

9. When the plant has been placed successfully in the medium, you will have to place the cup in the lid of the bucket. There is your system!

Modifications

You will be able to modify the system very easily. If you want, you could add a gauge to measure the water level. This can be done by cutting a half-inch hole on the side of the bucket and inserting a rubber tube of the very same size. Now, connect this tube to an elbow of half an inch and also install a tiny piece of tubing made of vinyl from the top of the bucket.

You could always link your system with a central reservoir or any other source of water using a rubber tube or a grommet. You will need to identify the right fitting methods for the modification.

You could also try to recreate the system by using a variety of materials that are dark in color and also hold a good quantity of water. You should also try to use a material that would help you create more space that would help in holding more plants.

Instructions

You will have to ensure that you monitor the level of water in the system while ensuring that the water level never drops to a point where the plants begin to suffer. You will need to add water to the plants begin to use up all the nutrient solution. When you add water to the bucket, you will need to continue to check the pH and make the adjustments. Make sure that you do not add any fertilizer to the bucket. If you add the fertilizer, you will contaminate the water leading to other problems. You will need to change the nutrient solution when the plants use the nutrient solution completely for the third time.

Ebb and Flow System

The Ebb and Flow system described in the previous chapter is an extremely easy to build and maintain. You will find that the design is extremely flexible and is automated. It is a known fact that plants that have been placed in a growing bed tend to hold a lot of water. The pump in this system is activated through a timer. When the pump is activated, it will pump the nutrient solution into the grow bed from the reservoir. The plants are all watered from the bottom of the reservoir or grow bed. The pump turns off when the plants have been watered for a few seconds. This is done four or five times a day. The system is extremely versatile and is extremely reliable. You will be able to handle the system and the plants really well.

Material needed

1. Air pump, air stone and air tubing
2. Water pump
3. Growing medium – clay or any other cheap medium like gravel
4. Fill and drain
5. Electric timer – 15 minute increments
6. Black irrigation tubing
7. Netted pots
8. Rubbermaid Black Storage Tote w/ Lid – 16 to 20 gallons
9. Rubbermaid Snap-toppers Clear Tote – 28 to 34 quart

10. Water & nutrient mix

Tools needed

1. Hole saw – 1 to ¼" holes

2. Drill bit – needed to drill ½" holes for water gauge and ¼" holes for air tubing

3. Tape measure – for the measurement of tubing sizes

4. Power drill – to cut holes in the lid

5. Teflon tape – for sealing bulkheads

6. Safety glasses

7. Knife – in case you don't have a drill machine

Construction

1. You will first need to cut two holes at the center of the tray that you have collected. You will need to smoothen the edges of the holes and then rub them against sandpaper to smoothen them perfectly. You have to ensure that the pots you make fit into the holes you have just made. You have to ensure that you have a rough estimate of the size of the hole in your mind before you make the holes.

2. When you have successfully cut the drain holes in the tray, you will need to place the tray over the tote lid. Make sure that the tray is at the center of the tote lid. You will need to mark the center of the holes you have created onto the lid. Make sure that you have marked it well. The idea is that the holes you have made and the drain fittings overlap each other properly.

3. You will now have to cut two more holes into the lid – one of these holes is for the pump plug and the other is to measure the level of the nutrient solution and also add more of the nutrient solution when the level of the solution falls.

4. You will now have to place the drain fittings into the holes that are at the center of the clear container. You will need to place the rubber gasket at the bottom of the bin and screw it in tightly. It is best to use your hands for this since tools make it extremely difficult to hold onto the screws tightly.

5. You will need to place the irrigation tube over the outlet fitting of the pump. The securing mechanism

is directly affected by the type of hosing you would be using in the system. It is possible that you may need to use a zip tie.

6. You will need to place the container that has been fitted with the drains in line with the holes that have been placed on the lids. You will need to do this since you will need to ensure that the parts all line up together perfectly. Now, place the lid firmly.

7. You will need to cut the tubing into a length that will help you lay the pump down at the bottom of the reservoir you will be using when the lid has been placed onto the reservoir. You will need to push the tubing right over the port from under the lid while using a zip tie to harness the entire set up.

8. You will need to place the air stone right at the bottom of the reservoir. You will also have to push the tubing through the access hole that you have made on the side of the reservoir. You will need to snap the top of the lid shut over the reservoir.

9. You will now have to use a piece of wood and create a dipstick. When you pour the water into the reservoir,

you will need to place the dipstick into the reservoir and measure the level of water while marking the dipstick. Make sure that you submerge the dipstick into the reservoir.

10. You will now need to add the water and also the nutrient solution to the reservoir. Make sure that the nutrient solution is concentrated. You will need to continue to adjust the pH. You will then need to add the water and plug in the air pump. This pump will help you diagnose if there are any mistakes in the system.

11. You will now have to take the pots and drill or cut a few holes around the sides of the pots. Now, add the growing medium to the pots.

12. You will need to plant the crops – vegetables, flowers or fruits – into the pots and move the medium all around the roots of the plant. This would ensure that the roots are not damaged. It is always good to start the planting with the pellets and also place them into the pot while ensuring that the roots have been submerged into the nutrient solution. You will need

to keep watching the plants well for the first few weeks.

System modifications

The ebb and flow system is easy to use since it helps in easy scaling. The system can be converted into businesses of smaller scales. This will make it extremely easy for you. The only disadvantage of using this system is that the size of the tray is a little tricky to estimate.

Instructions

When your plants have consumed half the nutrient solution, you will have to add more water to the reservoir to make sure that the initial level has gone back up. You will need to check the pH and adjust it accordingly. When the plants have begun to utilize the nutrient solution at a faster rate, you will need to drain them out and add another layer of the nutrient solution.

NFT System

The Nutrient Film Technique or the NFT system is one of the systems that have been sued widely when it comes to hydroponics or Aquaponics gardening. This is for the reason that you can have a larger scale of a garden. The NFT is made of a tube that holds the plants safely and provides them with the nutrient solution and also helps in letting the roots of the plants maintain contact with the solution. The technique that is used here is extremely flexible and helps you grow a wide range of plants! You will also be able to make a lot of modifications to the system if you want to. These modifications are endless since you could modify the size, layout or even the material you will be using.

The roots of the plants are all supposed to be grown in channels that are sealed, light – resistant and shallow. The nutrient solutions are all always swirling around the roots pretty much every hour of every day. This system obtained its name for the very fact that the system always requires the nutrient solution to flow around the roots and also helps the plants get the oxygen they would need.

The NFT system never uses any growing media that would mean that the moisture that would need to be held by the plants decreases constantly. This would mean that the plants begin to dry out soon. In order to overcome this problem, the system has a set of watering cycles that would ensure that the roots are always in contact with the roots of the plants. If you are a beginner, you will need to set a timer that would ensure that the water is pumped from the reservoir whenever you need it. The system has two channels that would help in circulating the nutrient solution all across the system. The reservoir is of extreme importance since the system always needs water to function and if there were no water, the pump would stop functioning.

Apart from using a water pump to help in the circulation of water throughout the system, the technique also uses the forces of gravity to assist the complete process. The ends of the PVC are all placed higher than the previous PVC. This is to ensure that the water enters the system at a height and then moves lower thanks to the gravitational forces of energy. The downward supports can be built easily using numerous types of material like PVC, lumber, etc. The support can also be hung from a stationary support that would ensure that the water returns to the system.

Material Needed

1. A 2 x 6 inch NFT stand or a 2 x 4 frame

2. 1 – 1 ½ inch wooden screws

3. 4 inch rubber end caps along with hose clamps

4. Rubber grommets

5. 4 inch PVC pipes of 10 inch lengths, cut into 3 portions

6. 4 straight connectors

7. 5 gallon bucket or container or Aquaponics fish tank

8. 1 x submersible pump

9. Air pumps, tubing & stones

10. 3 inch netted cups

11. ½ inch – ¾ inch irrigation tubing

12. Hydroponic nutrient

Tools needed

1. Utility knife

2. 3 inch hole saw

3. Screws Drill

4. Saw

5. Standard screwdriver

Construction

1. When you have decided on the type of container you would be using for the reservoir, you will need to start with the design for your stands. What you will need to remember is that the design of the stands must be done well to ensure that they are taller than the reservoir itself.

2. You will need to cut the lengths of the stand and cut a triangle out of the lengths. This is to ensure that the PVC can be held in a stable position. You will then need to join the lengths well using the other stands by placing them horizontally.

3. You will now have to drill a hole in order to make space for the tubing. This is to ensure that the tube connects to the caps well. You will need to drill these holes in the heights where you want the water to stay. You have to also ensure that the holes are at a height where you would be able to ensure that the water does not submerge the cups. You could also make the holes adjustable if you want to. This can be done by drilling a hole on the outside of the fitting in

order to adjust the level of water using the rubber fitting.

4. When you are purchasing the pump, you will need to ensure that it comes with an attachment that can be removed easily. This will be required since you will need to bind this to the piece of tubing in order to reach the top of the tube right from the bottom of the reservoir.

5. You will now need to push the tubes from the bottom to the NFT fitting through the created hole. You will need to use another piece of the tubing along with the NFT in order to reach the top of the tube. You will have to do the same with the bottom of the tube and the reservoir. You will now have to attach the caps together till they fit well on the pieces of the PVC.

6. The NFT system always runs well and if there are any leaks, you will be able to use the plumbing cement on the outside of the tubes. When looked from the perspective of toxicity, you will find that the plumbing cement is not the best one to use. It is only

good to use it on the outside of your system. You will find that you can conduct another leak test in an hour tops!

7. If you are someone who loves keeping every single item clean, you will need to sue a bleach solution to clean the reservoir and every other material before you drill any holes. This is to ensure that you maximize the flow that is within the tubes.

8. The next thing you will need to do is that you will need to drill the holes in the system that would be dependent on the type and the size of the plant. It is always good to make space for 6 – 9 plants. Make sure that you maintain at least 6inhches between each plant that you cultivate. You would do great by drilling the holes for the plants using the netter cups. You could also use plastic cups, but ensure that you are in a safe place. You will need to wear a mask to ensure that you do not harm yourself. You will need to remove all the dust off of the pipes.

9. You will need to make three holes in the lid covering the reservoir where each of the holes would have its

own purpose. You will need to use one for the supply of water, one for the drain and the other for the air tubing or the power cord.

10. You will need to leave the lid on top of the reservoir to ensure that the evaporation is reduced. You will also be able to protect your plants from any debris that may fall into the container.

11. You could choose to either use the netted pots that are available in the market or use the homemade netter pots. When you purchase them, you will be able to use the pots immediately. If you are making it at home, you will need to drill a lot of holes to ensure that the cups work well. You will need to make sure that the roots fit well through the holes in order to be submerged into the nutrient solution.

12. The lower part of the tubing must always be directed to that side of the reservoir where there is light – natural or artificial. You have to check the stands to ensure that you have the right orientation of the flow of water. The water needs to move from the top of the stands to the bottom and back into the reservoir.

13. When you have chosen a growing medium, you have to ensure that it is clean and has been sterilized well. This needs to be done to ensure that you do not contaminate the system with pests. If you are willing to purchase a medium from the store, you will only need to clean the dust or the debris.

14. When you are moving the plant from the soil into the reservoir, you will need to remove any soil particles from the plant. This is to avoid any clogging since that will harm the plants. Make sure that the plant is clean too.

Make sure that you place the taller plants at the back and the shorter ones in front to ensure that each plant receives the right amount of sunlight.

There are four factors that have an extreme influence on the workings of the NFT system.

- The number of plants
- The size of the channel tubing
- The specifications of the channel
- The capability of the pump

The best thing to do is to use a pump that is not too small. This is because of the fact that the solution may not be drained too easily. It would also affect the motor extremely badly. You will be able to transform the system extremely easily if you choose to. You can always experiment with the system in order to obtain the best out of it. You have learnt a great deal of the NFT system, but the modifications are always endless. You could always cut the tube into the same length to ensure that the plants have been fed well.

Thomas Thatcher

Chapter 7
Nutrient Solutions

Getting the correct nutrients to the roots of your plants roots is what hydroponics is all about. The science behind plant nutrition is quite complicated and at first can seem very daunting but it is not necessary to become a plant scientist to get to grips with what you will need to know in order to be a successful grower. It will, however, help to know some of the basics so you have an idea of what is going on and what all those chemicals are.

There are many different nutrients that a plant requires in order to grow and without which they will soon die. The three main nutrients are called macronutrients whilst an array of other nutrients are needed but in much smaller quantities.

The three-macro nutrients are:

Nitrogen (N): used in the production of chlorophyll and amino acids.

 Phosphate (P): used in the production of sugars, energy flowers and fruit.

Potassium (K): used in the production of sugars starch, roots and general hardiness.

These three components are always listed most prominently on bottles or packets of nutrients and given in numbers proportional to their quantity so if you were to see 15:9:12 you would know their proportions were fifteen percent Nitrogen, nine percent Phosphate and twelve percent Potassium. That would make up thirty six percent of the mix with the remainder being given over to water and micronutrients. It should be noted that the three figures are always given in the same order NPK although the percentage of each will vary according to its intended usage.

In hydroponics the nutrients most commonly supplied come in a powdered or a concentrated liquid form that you would then dilute according to instructions of the manufacturer. In my opinion, and that of many other growers, the liquid form is by far the most practical and easy to use.

As I have already mentioned the reservoir should be a tank that does not let in light so as to reduce the possibility of mold and algae build up. This reservoir should be at least the same size as the pots or tray that it is feeding and possibly bigger. Don't mix the nutrients in the reservoir but add them after premixing with water.

The pH level of your water is very important as it can have a detrimental effect on the nutrient take up if it is either too high or too low. Ideally you want it to be at between 5.5 and 7.0. Too much chlorine can also have adverse effects so that too will need to be dealt with. If you stand water in a bucket for twenty-four hours the chlorine will breakdown. Alternatively, you can buy distilled water that seems a bit of a waste of money to me or you can catch rainwater, which will be chlorine free and seems to me the most logical solution to the chlorine problem. Don't be too distracted by chlorine levels as they don't kill plants and water that has stood for twenty-four hours tends to be fine.

The pH is most commonly affected by the amount of calcium it contains. Too much calcium leads to hard water and a high pH. This will need to be tested with a pH tester and if it falls outside of the given range then you can add some drops of a chemical for raising it or another for lowering it depending on the reading you are getting. All hydroponic suppliers sell a two-part kit for raising and lowering pH. Simply dilute a few drops of one or the other in order to either raise or lower the pH to the required level. Do this mixing in a little at a time and then let the water settle before testing again. It is good to have a general idea of the pH of you water when you first start but after that most of the pH testing should be done after you have added the various nutrients, as these will further alter the pH levels. The digital testing devise, a bit like a thermometer, is quite cheap and simple to use.

One way to make your life easier is to have a second reservoir. One will be in use and the other will be full with just water. This will ensure that the water is at the same temperature so the plants don't have to deal with a sudden temperature change and will also mean you are free of any chlorine if using mains tap water. Try to always use tepid water at around 18°C but don't make this a major issue as you are going to have enough to get to grips with at the moment.

Once you have your water more or less pH neutral it is time to start mixing your nutrients and for the moment I am only going to deal with purpose bought hydroponic nutrients. They normally come in three parts that are mixed according to the manufacturer's instructions for the plants that you are growing. They tend to come with a chart for a range of plants and with a week-by-week dosage according to the age of the plants. In the beginning you will want to follow this chart quite closely but as your experience levels increase you will no doubt start experimenting with recipes of your own. Almost all hydroponic gardeners develop their individual recipes and start to add a series of additional products that they all swear are the best for the plants they hope to produce. I will get into some of those additives late but for now we will just stick to mixing of the basic three part nutrients.

Once you have the three bottles and have found the appropriate part of the chart that applies to your plants and the stage of growth they are at you will need to mix them. Don't just throw them all into a jar and shake them all up. In strong concentration they can react with one another and create an effect called blocking that inhibits their individual effectiveness. Instead place a few liters of water in a bucket that is the same size as your reservoir. This water will need to be chlorine free and to the correct pH. Of course if you have the second reservoir already prepared then that will be perfect. Pour the correct amount of the first nutrient into a measuring beaker and then pour it into the water. Now wash out the beaker and wait two minutes before repeating the procedure with the second nutrient. Finally repeat the process with the third nutrient. Remember it is important that you wash out the measuring beaker between nutrients to avoid blocking. It is also possible to purchase some cheap measuring syringes and use a separate one for each nutrient so as to avoid any possibility of mixing them up.

Once I have all my nutrients in the reservoir and I have waited a minute or two after adding the three then I give the reservoir a bit of a stir. At this stage I can retest my pH to ensure the levels are still within the accepted range of 5.5 to 7.0. It is likely that over time the pH will creep up slightly as the nutrients are drawn up by the plant. Because this is the case it would be good if you could keep the pH just slightly below neutral so if you can keep it to around 6.0 that would be ideal. I then also test my mix using another meter called a PPM meter or an EC meter and occasionally a TDC meter. Effectively they all do the same thing. They measure the salts in the nutrient mix. PPM stands for parts per million, EC stands for Electrical conductivity and TDS stands for total desired salts. This easy to use little gadget will be used often during the growing stage, as you will need to be constantly monitoring your nutrient mix to ensure the plant is getting all that it needs. Getting to grips with nutrient mixes is one of the trickiest parts of hydroponic gardening and I don't want to make it appear too complicated because you can generally learn all you need to by just following the chart that comes with the mixture. Remember that each producer will have a different recipe and so each system will vary slightly.

What you are trying to do with the plant varies at different times of its growth cycle and that is why the mixture of ingredients keeps altering. To start off you want plenty of nitrogen to bring the plants to a flowering stage as soon as possible. Later you will reduce the nitrogen but increase the phosphates to increase the flowering rooting and fruiting and all the way through the process you plant will be in need of small amounts of micronutrients. In the early days there will normally be a strong desire to add more nutrients in the hope that this will generate more and faster growth. In fact, too much nutrient can be worse for the plant than too little nutrient so if you must tamper with the manufacturers recommendations try to always err on the side of less rather than more.

Now you have got your reservoir to the pH you want and the nutrients to the level recommended by the manufacturer you are set to start pumping. Most systems require circulation at least twice a day and if you can get that up to once every two hours without water logging the plants that would be even better. You should be using your meter to check the nutrients every couple of days. If they start to get low then you can add a top up mix that is essentially a mild version of the mixes you are using without the micronutrients. The reason for this is that the plants use a lot of the macronutrients and only very little of the micronutrients. If you add more micronutrient it builds up in the system and becomes toxic to the plants. Outdoor units must not be exposed to rain that will dilute the water in the system.

Every two weeks you should replace the nutrient mix altogether. It is safe to pour the old mix onto any soil garden plants you have. Before making up the next mix clean out the reservoir with hot water or diluted bleach. You are then ready to start a new batch provided the water is chlorine free. This is also a good time to check the rest of the system to check that everything is working and there is no sign of algae. Pay particular attention to mist heads if you are using them as they are easily blocked up by micronutrient build up.

Although I have suggested checking your unit you should be checking your plants every day to ensure that they are strong and healthy and not showing any signs of stress. They will also let you know very quickly if there is any problem with the system. When you have harvested your crop then it is a good idea to strip the entire unit down and give everything a thorough cleansing. When you go a little ahead in this chapter, you will come across recipes you could use to make your nutrient solution and will also be able to identify the easiest ways to test the pH of the water in the reservoir.

The intricate nutrient solution

Before I move on to explain to you the intricacies of the nutrient solution, let me tell you a little about the strength of a plant. You could try to visualize the plant as a chain. The strength of the plant is similar to the strength of a chain. You may have come across the proverb, 'A chain is as strong as its weakest link'. This implies that your chain is always as strong if its links are all strong too! You will therefore have to ensure that every link is stable and has a good supply. You have to make sure that you only add the right quantity of the nutrients to the solution. You will also need to ensure that you understand your plants better since every plant will have a requirement of its own.

The nutrients that you will need are all available in the market and always come with a set of instructions about the proportions you will need to mix to obtain the final solution. You have to also understand what type of a solution you will need for your plant during the different stages of germination. You will find a ton of products in the market that you could use in the different systems of hydroponics. You may be a beginner and it may be easier for you to use the readymade solutions. But, if you choose to make nutrients for your plants, you could use the recipes at the end of the chapter to do the same!

When you have made a list of all the ingredients together, you will have to be careful about a few things. What is of great importance is that you need to design the solution in such a way that the hydroponics system works well. Make sure that you do not use any supplements at all in the system. This is because of the fact that the medium you use to grow your plants in do not have any microorganisms. Since they are not available, the nutrients from the supplements will not be transferred to the plants. You could choose to use certain powders if you want to, but ensure that they have multi purposes. Ensure that you use these powders only when there is extremely poor lighting.

If the location you have chosen to place your hydroponic system is under direct sunlight, ensure that you use a powder with at least two functions. This will ensure that the yield of the plants will multiply. This is because of an extremely simple reason. Multipurpose nutrients always ensure that they satisfy the needs of each one of your plants. You will be unable to bend the uses of the powders to satisfy the needs of one single plant. The second reason behind why it is good for you to use multipurpose nutrient powders is that blending the powders together would work best since that would imply that the plants have been given all the nutrients that they require. The best way to do this is by optimizing the growth of your plants by using this method.

There are a few people who would want to prepare their own nutrient solution. A few recipes have been given below and if want to prepare your own nutrients, you will need to follow these recipes word for word. These powders can be used at the different stages of germination.

Recipes for Nutrients

Let us look at a few recipes if you are keen on preparing your own nutrient solutions.

Vegetative Nutrient

Amount: 4 liters

Nitrogen: 38

Phosphorous: 24

Potassium: 48

Ingredients

- 24 lb. Calcium Nitrate
- 88 lb. Potassium Nitrate
- 122 lb. Sulfate of Potash
- 8 lb. Monopotassium Phosphate
- 10 lb. Magnesium Sulfate
- 4 lb. Fe Chelated Trace Elements

Instructions

Mix these ingredients separately and add the powder to four gallons of water.

Fruiting Nutrient

Amount: 4 liters

Nitrogen: 32

Phosphorous: 22

Potassium: 50

Ingredients

- 32 lb. Calcium Nitrate
- 10 lb. Potassium Nitrate
- 8 lb. Sulfate of Potash
- 6 lb. Monopotassium Phosphate
- 12 lb. Magnesium Sulfate
- 4 lb. Fe Chelated Trace Elements

Instructions

Mix these ingredients separately and add the powder to four gallons of water.

Flowering Nutrient

Amount: 4 liters

Nitrogen: 22

Phosphorous: 32

Potassium: 74

Ingredients

- 20 lb. Calcium Nitrate
- 10 lb. Potassium Nitrate
- 4 lb. Sulfate of Potash
- 8 lb. Monopotassium Phosphate
- 10 lb. Magnesium Sulfate
- 2 lb. Fe Chelated Trace Elements

Instructions

Mix these ingredients separately and add the powder to four gallons of water.

The secrets behind the chelated trace elements

The chelated trace elements have an amazing combination that is unique. The first thing for you to do is to understand these combinations since that will ensure that you make the right combination of the nutrient solution if that is what you want to do. You will need to ensure that the combination is right since an excess would harm the plants in ways you would never have imagined.

1. Molybdenum – 0.06%
2. Manganese – 2%
3. Copper – 0.1%
4. Iron – 7%
5. Zinc – 0.4%
6. Boron – 1.30%

General instructions

When you have decided to make the nutrient solutions for your hydroponics system on your own, you will need to follow a few instructions that are extremely important. Please read this section carefully to go over those rules.

The first thing you will need to do is to fill the reservoir or two reservoirs with extremely clean and hot water. You will only have to fill the reservoir to three fourths of the capacity.

Now, add the nutrients that have been given above in the recipes. Make sure that you add them one after the other since that way you will be able to ensure that the nutrients have mixed well with the system. This is extremely important.

Make sure that you remember the fact that the salts are in their native states that would mean that there is a possibility of them having a strong reaction. You will need to keep yourself protected well. Ensure that you always follow the instructions that have been given for every nutrient you will be using.

How do you test the pH of the nutrient solution?

When you are adding the nutrient solution to your reservoir, you will have to ensure that you measure the pH of the solution. You could use two techniques – TDS (Total Dissolved Solids) and PPM (Parts Per Million) – for the same. You would have come across the term electrical conductivity that is the very same thing. I have said this since you will be measuring the electrical conductivity of the nutrient solution that you have made.

You could use multiple ways to analyze and measure the PPM of any nutrient solution. The simplest way to do this is by using a digital PPM gauge. In order to take the measurement, you will need to place the gauge in the solution. The best part of this is that you do not have to calibrate the gauge. If you always change the nutrient solution the concentration and the pH are always at the level needed. The best thing for you to do is to follow every instruction that has been given on the back of the nutrient you will be using. It is always good to replace the solution at least once every three weeks if you are keen on obtaining good results.

It is an absolute waste to have a nutrient solution in the reservoir if you find that that the plant cannot absorb the nutrients easily. In order to understand the ability of a plant to absorb all the nutrients that are in the solution, you will have to gauge the pH of the nutrient solution. It is always measured on a scale of 1 -14 and always represents the number of hydrogen ions in the nutrient solution. The pH is always good to try to understand the nature of the solution – whether or not it is basic or acidic. If the scale is one you will find that the concentration of the hydrogen ion is extremely low, while if it is a seven it means that the solution is neutral. If the scale says 14, you will find that the solution is alkaline or basic. You could also use a simple litmus test if you want, just how you did it in chemistry class.

To Recap

By now you may be starting to feel like you have been bombarded with a little too much information especially if hydroponics is something you have never dealt with before. The whole idea is to ensure that you get a nutrient rich liquid to the roots of your plants with a nearly neutral pH. If you focus on those priorities you won't go too far wrong. To do this you will need an EC meter for the salts or nutrients and a pH meter. You can buy fairly inexpensive units that do both measurements for you so checking the levels is not difficult. You should be checking your mixture once a day. Small scale units tend to fluctuate more than larger ones so the home grower has to be just as alert to changes as the large scale producer.

In the event of pH getting too high or too low then add a few drops of the appropriate product after diluting. There are two products you can buy for this and they clearly state that they are either for raising or lowering the pH. You should not try to change the pH more than 0.5 in either direction in one day as you may shock the plants. As you started with the right pH balance larger changes are unlikely.

The EC meter will give you a reading of the conductivity of the water based on the amount of salts that it contains. Aim for a level of between 1.2 and 2.0. If it goes above this you can dilute the mix by adding water and if it goes below then you can top it up with top up according to the manufacturer's instructions. I hope that simplifies this chapter for you.

Chapter 8
What to Grow

One of the great advantages of hydroponics is the wide variety of crops that you can grow. In many ways the choice is endless but you do need to take into consideration the constraints imposed on you by the size of your unit and the space that it is in. If you are a large producer in a greenhouse set up you will probably want to concentrate on a small range of crops that sell easily and if you are a home grower working in an apartment then perhaps it is best to focus on just the crops that you buy most of. For the small producer a good place to start is always with lettuce as it is a salad crop that is eaten by ninety percent of westerners on a daily basis. It is also a crop that takes up little space and really tastes better freshly picked. In addition you can also harvest enough leaves for a salad whilst leaving the plant to continue growing.

The second most popular crop is tomato. If there is one crop that tastes better than all others when picked and eaten immediately then it has to be the tomato. There are hundreds of varieties so choose one that you think you will enjoy and that takes up not too much space. If possible grow two plants of different varieties that will produce at different times so that you can harvest for a longer period. If you are combining your hydroponics with grow lights and growing indoors then it is possible to have tomatoes virtually all year round.

Cucumbers are another plant that can be very rewarding. In an indoor environment go for a dwarf variety and have a frame up which they can climb.

Peppers are not only easy to grow they also make surprisingly attractive plants especially if they are the brightly colored varieties. Another crop we use on a regular basis in our homes so an instant saving there.

Spinach is one of the most popular leaf vegetables and is very high in vitamins and iron. These days there are many varieties ranging from those with small rounded leaves through to the more traditional longer leaved ones. All of them can have some leaves harvested whilst leaving the parent plant to continue growing and reproducing new leaves.

For fruit strawberries are one of the best fruit for the hydroponic producer in both the private and commercial environments. With the vastly extended growing season you will have, the potential for good economic returns are high.

Blue berries are going through a major popularity boom at the moment because of their high levels of antioxidants that have proven health benefits. They like an acid soil when growing in the ground and as it is so easy to control acidity in a hydroponic production unit this makes them solid candidates for both home and commercial production.

Herbs can be surprisingly expensive when you actually work out what quantities you get when you buy them in a supermarket. Growing your own makes sense and even if you are only intending to grow enough for you and your family it is possible that you may find that you are producing more than you can eat. If you ask around it is highly likely that you will find ready buyers amongst your family and neighbors. Basil is used in a number of recipes as an addition to salads. It is also high in antioxidants. A very easy to grow herb, it costs a small fortune in supermarkets when you look at the price per kilogram.

The other really easy to grow herb is coriander. With its many health benefits and multiple culinary uses this is a versatile crop that you can be harvesting within four weeks and which can easily provide two and sometimes three crops per year.

Chapter 9
Pests and Diseases

There is one sure thing about any form of gardening and that is that you will always run into problems with pests and disease at some stage or other. In the case of hydroponics the problem of pests is reduced considerably because your crop is not growing in the soil where many bugs tend to lay their eggs and hibernate. Unfortunately, that still does not mean that you will be totally immune to receiving attention from nasty creatures as those healthy looking leaves and fruit will be just too much for them to resist and they will find other ways of getting at an easy meal.

One of the most important lessons any gardener learns is that of observation. Bugs and insects have developed various defense mechanisms and the main one is the ability to blend into their environment so that they can go unnoticed for as long as possible. Another survival strategy is to breed very rapidly. The gardener needs to almost cultivate a sixth sense when it comes to spotting pests. A casual glance will see only a healthy looking lettuce but the trained eye will soon spot one or two tiny aphids lurking hidden beneath the leaves. If they are dealt with swiftly then the problem has been averted but left to their own devices those few aphids can breed to almost plague proportions within a matter of days and suddenly you whole harvest is at risk and getting rid of them now demands all-out war. Take the time to look closely at your plants, turning over leaves and using a magnifying glass if you need to. Also learn to recognize when a plant is not looking one hundred percent healthy and is displaying even the slightest signs of stress.

Here are some of the most common pests you are likely to encounter.

Mealy Bug

An oval shaped scale insect that sucks sap from the veins of leaves. They produce a sticky substance known as honey dew that often gives away their presence. They can be dealt with by wiping with rubbing alcohol on a cotton ball or spraying with an insecticidal soap.

Spider Mites

These tiny insects are almost invisible to the naked eye and they thrive in green house conditions. You often only become aware of them when you see a fine web covering the underside of leaves and the base of leaves starts to become a mottled brown as they suck out the chlorophyll. In small infestations caught early they may be destroyed simply by misting the leaves with a mild soapy solution. Use vegetable based insecticidal soap if they get out of control.

Thrips

Small winged insects a little larger than the head of a pin and they too like to suck sap. Leaves become distorted and loose color. They are best dealt with by spraying with soapy water.

Aphids

There are various types of aphid but they all have one thing in common and that is that they can breed really fast. It is estimated that if all the offspring from a single aphid were to survive for a year then their combined body weight would be sufficient to throw the earth out of orbit. Fortunately for us they are quite fragile creatures and if you spot them early they can be dealt with before we go spinning off toward another universe. They are sapsuckers and tend to favor the tips of green leaves. They are easily destroyed by a quick blast of soapy spray.

This is a very short list of some of the most common pests but there are many more and many varieties of the ones that I have listed. What I was trying to emphasize is that they are easy to deal with if you catch them early. Given that most of the plants you are growing are likely to be edible then you need to decide if you are going to treat your pests with chemicals or organic treatments. Organic pest control tends to be cheaper and as I don't want to expose myself to any more toxic chemicals than I need to I tend to opt for them. There is, however, a vast array of chemical sprays and treatments on the market that are highly effective at killing any pest you care to mention and you only have to go into a garden center and describe your problem and you will be offered a selection of arms with which to respond.

On the organic front the arsenal is more limited but here are some of the treatments that have worked perfectly well for me.

Insecticidal soaps can be sprayed from an ordinary spray bottle and are my weapon of choice. You can purchase them or make up your own using any number of recipes off the net using common household ingredients.

Neem oil is produced from an evergreen tree that originates in India and is now grown widely around the world. Its oil is prized by both the organic gardening and cosmetic industry. It will be available at most nurseries or online.

Nettle tea. This is a product that any gardener who has access to nettles can make himself. Simply steep a large handful of nettles in lightly simmering water for five minutes then filter the greenish brown liquid into a spray bottle. It gets more powerful as it ages and is a great insect deterrent but beware, as it does smell.

On the disease front the main threat comes from high humidity and the close density of planting that is common in the hydroponic system. This makes growers, particularly greenhouse producers, susceptible to molds and mildews of which there are many. The secret is to increase ventilation as much as possible and to reduce humidity down to the lowest levels your plants will accept.

Both pests and disease are reduced if you practice good garden hygiene. Remove and throw away dead plants and leaves immediately. Thoroughly clean and disinfect all equipment between crops as well as green houses. Use tools specifically for the hydroponic system so as to avoid unintentionally carry in disease spores from other plants in the garden. If you are using grow lights then don't be tempted to share the light with other house plants that you may have as you risk transfer problems.

Chapter 10

What are the Benefits of Hydroponic Gardening?

Numerous people have started to work towards hydroponic gardening instead of using conventional methods of gardening. The only problem that you may have with this sort of arrangement is that the plants may not have the ability to keep themselves free of pests. You have been given a detailed explanation on how you can get rid of the pests if you find your system affected by them.

It has been seen that people all across the world have started to become extremely conscious about the food they are consuming. They have started to consume organic food. Here is the thing: not all organic food is good since you will not be able to know the method of cultivation that has been used. There are numerous people who have always stated that they have produced organic food when in reality they are producing regular food – that is food with pesticides and fertilizers. This is because of the fact that they will begin to focus on the returns they will be obtaining. You will need to be extremely careful when you are purchasing the organic food.

When you switch over to using a hydroponics system instead of using the conventional farming method, you will find that you cannot cheat at all. You have to ensure that you do not use even one chemical in your system since that will affect the growth of all the plants in the system. If you begin to use any pesticides or fertilizers in your system, the plants in the reservoir will begin to wither. Make sure that you do not have even one chemical for this very reason. The best part is that you will be able to produce organic food since you are never allowed to use any chemicals, even if they are organic!

The most important thing you will need to keep in your mind is that the hydroponics system does not need any chemical at all to function well. The system works towards creating a harmony between the different elements of nature. The fertilizers you provide to the plants in your system are all natural and found in the nutrient solution. This will ensure that your plants grow very well.

Other Benefits

Let us look at a few other benefits that you will obtain when you use hydroponic systems.

Farming

The greatest benefit of all is that you will obtain a great deal of knowledge on effective techniques of farming. You will be able to obtain a yield that is either thrice or four times the yield you may obtain when you try to use the conventional methods of farming.

When you begin to use the land you own to cultivate your plants traditionally, you will find yourself wasting a lot of water. The water that you will use to cultivate your plants would often be used to clean the soil and will end up seeping deep into the soil. An extremely minute amount of water is absorbed by the roots of your plant. You could probably be wondering why I am saying this since you would be using a lot of water in the hydroponic system. The fact is that the water in the system is always circulated around the roots of the plant that would ensure that the water never goes to waste.

You will find that you do not have the need to pull any weeds out of the hydroponic system since every plant always grows extremely well since the medium used in the system is extremely controlled. The plants in the hydroponic system always grow faster than the plants that have been cultivated using traditional techniques. This is always due to the fact that the nutrient solution that contains every mineral and vitamin your plant needs. This would imply that you do not have to work hard or even spend a lot of money! You only need to have the right proportions of the nutrients before you pour it into the reservoir.

Environment

Fertilizers and pesticides have tons of chemicals in them that would often lead to harming the ground water, which is because of the fact that the chemicals seep through the ground. This would lead to polluting the larger water bodies that are connected to the ground water table. When you start using a hydroponic system at home, you will find that you do not need any fertilizers and pesticides. This is because of the fact that you will be using a nutrient solution to keep all your plants healthy. The food you obtain thereof is extremely important.

The other aspect to consider about the environment is the land. People have been using all the land they can find! When you use a hydroponic system, you will be able to conserve a lot of pieces of land. This is because of the fact that you will need extremely small amounts of space to start and maintain your hydroponic system.

Health

The plants that have been cultivated in the system are extremely healthy. There are no chemicals that are inserted in the system that would mean that the plants are chemical free. The only way the plants obtain their health is through the nutrient solutions that are made. The organic fertilizers are often obtained from animals, which contain a certain pathogen that would harm the plants extremely badly.

Thomas Thatcher

Chapter 11
Grooming of the Plants

People are always worried about how they can make sure that their plants are healthy and do not become prey for certain pests and insects. This is when they, including you, will need to learn a little something about grooming. There are four techniques to grooming your plants. You have to use these methods carefully in order to ensure that you do not hurt the delicate plants. It is a fact that the plants that grow in the system are delicate although they are strong to handle any climatic changes. This however, does not mean that your plants will be attacked by a variety of pests. You may make mistakes initially, but that is alright since you will begin to learn from those mistakes. Make sure that you keep yourself motivated and are forging ahead in your journey.

Pinching

This is an extremely simple technique and it is essential that you are extremely careful with the delicate plants. You have to use your thumb and forefinger to hold the part of the plant you will be cutting gently but firmly. This method will help you keep all your plants compact and extremely clean and neat. You will always be able to use this method to retain the structure of the plant. You have to always keep in mind that you pinch above a node since you do not want to harm your plant. You could use this method for plants that have a very soft stem. If you cannot use this method, you will need to use the next method.

Pruning

Make sure that the pruner shears that you will be using to trim all the edges of the plants are sharp. This is because of the fact that the stems you will be cutting are wood. You will have to use the prunes to get rid of any parts of the plant that have been injured, even if it is a small injury, you will need to remove that part. Make sure you do this to avoid giving your plants any diseases. During the spring season, you will need to do this more frequently since your plants will begin to grow extremely fast!

Deadheading Flowers

If there are any dry or dead flowers or even dry leaves, you will need to remove them. This is to avoid the growth of mold, which often causes and spreads numerous diseases.

Cleaning

Make sure that you always keep your hydroponic system extremely clean. It is only when there is no dust in the system will you be able to attract the right amount of sunlight which will keep your plants strong and will help them grow well. Ensure that you clean your leaves and flowers using a damp cloth. Also ensure that you are extremely gentle!

Tips and Tricks!

When you decide to use a hydroponics system at home, you will be looking for ways to make your life easier. This section will thrill you since it holds a treasure of tips that will help you through your journey. You may be overwhelmed at times when you find that there are multiple things you will need to remember and take care of while you are working on the system. Worrying only makes it worse! All you need to do is enjoy what you are doing and you will be perfectly fine!

1. You have to ensure that the equipment you will be using for the system has been washed well before it is placed in the hydroponics system. Make sure that no dirt enters the system since that makes it a little more work for you. You will need to remove the dirt and then use the system.

2. When you are trying to identify the different media you can use in the hydroponics system, the first thing you will need to check is the pH. Make sure that the medium does not cause any fluctuations in the pH of the system since that would affect the plants adversely.

3. When you are trying to analyze the water in your surroundings, you will probably find that the water contains too much protein. This will need to be removed immediately before you use it in your system.

4. You need to ensure that the nutrient solution you make always has the right quantity of minerals and vitamins. If you have too much of the nutrients, you will be affecting the growth of the plants. The same can be said for a low amount of nutrients in the solution.

5. You need to remember to always use products made from nature. This is to ensure that chemicals do not make their way into your hydroponics system. If they enter the system then they will be absorbed by the plants that would harm them internally.

6. It is ossible that your plants could be affected by a variety of pests. These need to be removed soon to avoid harming your plants or the entire system. You could always use a spray made of water and vinegar that you can use on your plants if you find them affected by pests.

7. If you have any plants out in the open, you have to ensure that there is a protective covering over them. You will be able to keep them from any harm they may come across if they are out in the open. You will

also be able to keep them away from the birds and other pests.

Chapter 12

The Requirements for a Hydroponics System

The hydroponics systems are always easy to use and are extremely easy to develop. There are a few conditions and requirements that will need to be met by a hydroponics system in order to obtain a high yield. You have been given a list of all these conditions in order to recall them easily.

- You have to ensure that the pH of the nutrient solution lies between the values 5.8 – 6.5 while the electrical conductivity must lie between the values 1.5 - 2.5. If every plant is subjected to these conditions, the yield will be very high. If there were a sudden change, it would harm the plants in the system terribly.

- It is extremely vital that you monitor the temperature of the nutrient solution in the tank. When the temperature increases, the rate of respiration also increases which would increase the demand for oxygen. If you place the hydroponics system in a greenhouse, you will find that the temperature has increased too much and is at its peak in the afternoon!

- There will be a lot of oxygen that has been dissolved in the nutrient solution in order to ensure that the roots of the plants can absorb it. If there is a reduced amount of oxygen it will mean that the rate of absorption has also decreased. This will have a direct impact on the yield of the crops. If the system is closed, you will find that the collection of the nutrient solution will allow for the aeration of the tank.

- If you are using root-dipping techniques, you will need to give way for an air gap that is nominal. This will need to be measure with respect to the nutrient solution. The roots will be absorbing the oxygen for the plants and will help the plants grow well together in the same system.

- You have to make changes to the nutrient solution, but ensure that you do not make sudden changes since that will affect the growth of the plants.

- When the crop is growing, you will find that the concentration of the ions is decreasing in the nutrient solution. You will find that the decrease of the ions is inversely proportional to the nutrient solution level. If there is an increase, you will find that it is not healthy for the plants. You will need to remove the solution and add the newer solution to the reservoir.

- Since you are growing plants in a medium without soil, you will need to ensure that there is adequate light.

- Any seedlings that can be used to avoid pests and diseases will need to be used when you are trying to establish the hydroponics crops. You will have to remove any plant if it has been infected or harmed. If you do not do this, you will be inviting pests to your system.

- If you come across a nematode problem when you use solid media, you will need to empty the system – remove the plants and the media. You will now have to sterilize the media and replace it if you still doubt the quality of the media. You have to also ensure that there are no nematodes in the water.

- Algae will begin to develop in the system as time passes and will tend to block the passageway making it difficult for the system to provide the plants with the nutrient solution. In order to avoid such a problem, you will need to use dark shades of pipes and also maintain an extremely clean system. Also make sure that the solution has absolutely no chlorine in it.

- You have to make sure that you have a good amount of spacing between the crops you will be placing in the reservoir. This is to ensure that each plant gets its fair share of nutrients.

- You will need to make sure that there is an adequate amount of nutrients that are needed to maintain the yield of the crops. You have to therefore, ensure that every plant gets a little bit of each of these elements. You will need to ensure that the nutrient solution is in the right amount since that is the only way you will be able to ensure a better yield.

Thomas Thatcher

Conclusion

I hope that some of the technicalities here have not put you off what can be a very rewarding field of horticulture. In the beginning it may seem a little overwhelming but as you start to work with the different systems and methods you will find that you begin to get a feel for the subject. In gardening terms this is still a fairly new method and we are all still learning as the system evolves. There are some really cheap and easy methods for you to experiment with and once you have seen how straightforward hydroponics really is and how much bigger a yield can be achieved then I am sure you will want to move up to greater things. This system is already being used to produce many of the crops we buy at the supermarket and eat on a day to day basis and there is no reason why you should not be doing some of that production for your own home and perhaps from there even looking to expand toward bigger things.

Thank you for Reading! I Need Your Help...

Dear Reader,

I Hope you Enjoyed "**Hydroponics: Hydroponics Gardening Guide - from Beginner to Expert**". I have to tell you, as an Author, I love feedback! I am always seeking ways to improve my current books and make the next ones better. It's readers like you who have the biggest impact on a book's success and development! So, tell me what you liked, what you loved, and even what you hated. I would love to hear from you, and I would like to ask you a favor, if you are so inclined, would you please share a minute to review my book. Loved it, Hated it - I'd just enjoy your feedback. As you May have gleaned from my books, reviews can be tough to come by these days and you the reader have the power make or break the success of a book. If you'd be so kind to review the book

https://www.amazon.com/review/create-review?ie=UTF8&asin=B01BCNV4VW,

I would greatly appreciate the support! Thank you so much again for reading "**Hydroponics: Hydroponics Gardening Guide - from Beginner to Expert**" and for spending time with me! I will see you in the next one!

Thomas Thatcher

Check Out More From The Publisher...

Social Media: Master Social Media Marketing - Facebook, Twitter, YouTube & Instagram
By Grant Kennedy
http://www.amazon.com/Social-Media-Marketing-Facebook-Instagram-ebook/dp/B018Y68SWS

Survival: The Survival Guide for Preppers, Make Yourself Ready Through Hunting, Fishing, Canning, and Foraging
By Jack Campbell
http://www.amazon.com/Survival-Preppers-Permaculture-Bushcraft-Hydroponics-ebook/dp/B01573FBP8

Krav Maga: Dominating Solutions to Real World Violence
By George Silva
http://www.amazon.com/Krav-Maga-Dominating-Solutions-Violence-ebook/dp/B01A2BL6CW

Gardening: Hydroponics for Beginners: The Ultimate Guide to Hydroponic Gardening
By Melissa Honeydew
http://www.amazon.com/Hydroponics-Sufficiency-Vegetables-Homesteading-Preservation-ebook/dp/B01508IZAS

Gut: The Key to Ultimate Health - SIBO, IBS & Fatigue
By Maria Lexington
http://www.amazon.com/Healthy-Living-Happiness-Schizophrenia-Fibromyalgia-ebook/dp/B010KM9CLA